The End of Travel

The End of Travel

✳

Julie Bruck

Brick Books

CANADIAN CATALOGUING IN PUBLICATION DATA

Bruck, Julie, 1957–
The end of travel

Poems.

ISBN 1-894078-04-7

I. Title.

PS8553.R8225E52 1999   C811'.54   C99-931969-8
PR9199.3.B78E52 1999

We acknowledge the support of the Canada Council for the Arts
for our publishing programme. The support of the Ontario Arts
Council is also gratefully acknowledged.

Cover image is courtesy Squarebooks,
from *Spanning The Gate* (hand-coloured by Ann Rhoney).
Author photo is by Nina Bruck.

Typeset in Ehrhardt. The stock is acid-free Zephyr Antique laid.
Printed and bound by The Porcupine's Quill Inc.

Brick Books
431 Boler Road, Box 20081
London, Ontario, N6K 4G6

brick.books@sympatico.ca

Contents

for
Paul McGoldrick
&
Phoebe Tallman

We'd rather have the iceberg than the ship,
although it meant the end of travel.
— Elizabeth Bishop
The Imaginary Iceberg

One minute there was road beneath us and the next just sky.
— Ani DiFranco
Out of Range

I.

Dividing the Dark

✳

It's rare, slow as a creaking of oars,
and she is so frail and short of breath
on the street, the stairs – tiny, Lilliputian,
one wonders how they do it.
So, wakened by the shiftings of their bed nudging
our shared wall as a boat rubs its pilings,
I want it to continue, before her awful
hollow coughing fit begins. And when
they have to stop (always), until it passes, let
us praise that resumed rhythm, no more than a twitch
really, of our common floorboards. And how
he's waited for her before pushing off
in their rusted vessel, bailing when they have to,
but moving out anyway, across the black water.

> 'I felt as if I was being kidnapped,
> even if I wasn't.'
>   – Elizabeth Bishop

Imagine Elizabeth six years old,
being torn from this narrow province,
a train's headlamp dividing the dark, south-west,
all the way to Worcester, Massachusetts, 1916.
Our bus flies down the same curved road,
past the sign for Pictou County, and a yellow
diamond warning magically of *Flying Stones*.
The skies are wild and northern. I can still
hear the aggrieved honking of the Canada goose
I disturbed this morning in the Wildlife Management Area,
and now, by the sign ordering us to *YEILD*
in the late half-light, I almost expect
Miss Bishop's lonely moose, high as a church,
homely as a house, to appear at the next bend.
Our driver waves to every passing truck.
Their headlights flash across a farmhouse window,
redden the eye of a roadside dog.
One trucker doffs his cap as he roars past,
going home to his invisible house by the water,
where five pennies buys you a great many humbugs,
where the dress was all wrong. She screamed.
The child vanishes. Where the moon
in the bureau mirror looks out a million miles.

DIAGNOSIS

When I replace the dangerous receiver,
a baby in the neighbouring apartment
tries its new, unequivocal lungs.

Someone I love will need two
strong men to lift him soon,
from his bed to a chair in the light.

The news seeps through my address book
with its alphabetized individuals, whose only
revisions have been marriages or moves.

It snakes among the clothes I sort,
fresh from the spin cycle, the way,
even wet, they hold the body's shape.

It sears the air when the phone rings,
freights it when no one calls, and shines
on the waxy leaves of the philodendron,

which no matter how neglected, spills
new vines onto the floor, and whose blind,
stupid, furled green heads, lift themselves.

1948 is what my father wrote on the back
of the black-and-white photo with the scalloped edge.
He lies in a hammock, T-shirt and chinos,
a young, handsome man slung between birches;
one hand grips the edge of the hammock,
the other circles his infant son.

My father's face is an open grin.
That dark mass is just our fat, benign
dachshund, asleep as always, in the grass.
My brother, who is fifty now, and sometimes,
missing, turns his eyes to the camera,
but buries his cheek in my father's side.

My brother's baby-arm is raised,
as if to shield himself from a blow.
There were no blows. Someone
may have asked him to wave at the camera.
The air is a warm scrim of leaf-light. My brother
doesn't like requests. And he doesn't wave.

ADULT CHILDREN

Something in their house is always broken,
and my parents keep speeding off for parts.
Hey, where 'ya going? we call after them,
up to our necks in swimming pool water.
The powerful car disturbs the gravel;
the gravel quiets again.

Hey! we keep calling, our voices
softened by leafy shadow and water.
By then, their car has joined the highway,
but we're laughing so hard we can't
yell anymore, can only reach into thin air
with the arms we had as children.

What will they do for lunch? I ask J.,
whose parents died before he was twenty,
leaving him few instructions,
and nothing to separate from.
Those kids, he says, shaking his head,
until our laughter makes the water tremble,
the yellow house fragment.

I can hear them coming from too
far away, know exactly how the dark car
will slice past the birches, sun on chrome
and on their silver heads, bringing
appliance parts or bread or fresh news.
I am thirty-six years old; my head's above
water and I am holding my breath.

A boy kills himself at fifteen,
and it takes his sister most of a life
to emerge from those deep waters,
something always sucking her under.

She'd just begun to slip
out of that old, wet dress
when she wrote her brother an elegy,
offering him rest:

There is a raft in the centre
of my chest, she wrote
before she or anyone else knew
what flowered in her lung.

It's a beautiful poem, we said,
It's finished, and we turned
to other matters. *Climb on,*
she'd written, *Make use of me.*

One more tumour in one more friend:
The river we drink. Whether he finished
recording the album, which was emotionally
difficult, or if she ever came to terms
with her father or ex-husband – difficult, also.
How local Belugas beach themselves
weekly, their brains marinated in chemicals
we can't pronounce, or clean as they were
at birth – depending on who's talking.
We talk about that well-groomed woman
who sits on her bench every morning, pointing
at passersby, screaming in a German accent,
You! Your life is ending. We're talking
our heads off, because it's the only
tune we know, mouths forming the shape
of *green leafy vegetables, a virus may
cause heart attack, exercise more or less,
free radicals, free will,* reciting the litany
of round-the-clock *care-giving* like some
kind of mutant prayer, as one of us steps
off the curb in traffic, and the other
catches hard on her coat sleeve and pulls.

II.

Kate's Dress

✳

CATASTROPHE

The city was still asleep and I dreamed
myself awake: the huge silver plane fell,
nose-first, like a slow, thick arrow.
It slid behind the cut-out skyline, simple
as that. The sky went blank as a screen.

No sound of impact, and afterwards,
a deeper silence. Who else saw the plane
sink, as if this were part of the flight plan?
Whom should I alert? A door opens
and closes, as it does every morning.

Under my window, two restaurant workers
share a smoke before the breakfast crowds.
I want to call out, say something must be done,
but they're laughing in a foreign language.
I should have known then. I knew.

Some beauty will be born of this,
said my friend's blind mother
across the hospital cafeteria table
hours after the doctor said
inoperable and closed her daughter up.
All morning we'd drifted in and out
of the flower-sweetened room,
watching the morphine drip, taking
Kate's hand, holding her gaze.

I don't know about beauty, I said
and got up to order our lunch
from two women who'd been a comfort all week,
their small Scottish kindnesses a balm.
We ate our egg salads on whole wheat
as though we'd never tasted real food –
the creamy sweetness of the filling, surprise
bite of green onion – and drank Diet Cokes
until we'd washed our mouths clean.

I loved everything about our lunch –
the newsprint placemats with their oily spots,
crumbs on the unbreakable plates,
and especially the metal napkin dispenser
recently replenished by someone's deft hand
with what the Scottish women would call
serviettes, *Help yourselves, dearie,* in that burr.
I loved the hospital employees on break,
smoking outside the window, jousting
and flirting with their serviceable bodies.

I loved Edgar Jones, the deaf man
interviewed on the radio last night –
a music archivist who says it doesn't
matter if he can't hear anymore: he still
feels the way he did when he first heard Sibelius,
It's in my heart, you understand?
I loved Kate's mother's lined, outdoor face,
the loose wisps of white hair
framing her fine bones, the lively, blue,
unseeing eyes. I loved the shed paper
skin of the plastic straw, the way
the straws rose slowly in the Coke cans
and we pushed them back down to drink.

I loved the terra cotta walls around us,
freshly painted by people who'd done
their job adequately; loved the moment
someone decided to place the poster
of a whitewashed Greek village *there*,
and not an inch higher or lower.
I wanted to eat all my meals in the hospital
cafeteria, each bite a tiny explosion.
I don't know about beauty, I said.

GREENE AVE.

Montreal's blazing in tufts
of acid green and crabapple pink.
Clouds mass at dusk behind
Mount Royal like additional summits,
as my father noted yesterday
from his favourite chair, pleased
as he should be with the rented view.

Framed by my office window,
two elderly women in pink suits
with matching handbags and shoes,
twin iced confections, swirl
across the parking lot to lunch.

It rains, the sun comes out;
a young girl in white begins
her slow, meditative dance
around each parked car.
The pastel ladies reappear, fold
their legs into the Seville.

Alone in their vacant space,
the girl in white spins and spins.
A man pees behind a parking meter,
hails a cab with his free hand.
The cab pulls over, the cab
will wait, and that ring is my rented phone.
Anything to be that girl, turning.

LISTENING TO MORPHINE

The doctors say days, maybe
a week, and we've been draping
wet washcloths over Kate's feet, the only
part of her that can still stand touch.
The chimney isn't ready, she says,
not ready for a fire. Thanks,
I can't finish mine – that's enough.

From this high hospital window,
it is still August, early evening,
one of those perfect Sundays
with that sudden scent of fall.
We have to have chicken, that's all
there is to it. Who are they, the RCMP?

The vertical blinds sway like blown wheat.
Way down, a small boy with golden hair –
I skated with Lyle Lovett today, sends
his regards – is hosing his bicycle off
in a driveway, and the intermittent music
of water splashing warm pavement
is a sweetness impossible to bear.

But an argument breaks out at the house
next door, with someone screaming
on the front steps and a dog
frantically humping someone else's leg.
A car pulls up with a boom box
to add its two cents; in the room
the nurse sets the morphine higher.

Time again for ice and towels,
to check the nursing station clock.
In an hour, I'll leave her as I do
every evening, whisper, *see ya soon,*
while my hand digs for keys. I will walk
out of here, go home and write this down.
And if I decide to, I can change it.

Last night, going to the metal closet
for foot lotion, I saw the red dress
she'd worn in here – just for tests – held
by its thin wire hanger, and below,
her straw bag and sandals, uneven wear
on the heels, insoles burnished by her feet.
It seemed one sleeve of the dress had just
dropped the straw bag and would soon
sweep it up again, because the light
was changing, because it was time,
and there were errands before the traffic,
or she'd just stopped in, because
we were always stopping in on the way
somewhere else, that breathless exchange
at departure – the feel of her narrow shoulders
through the red dress, before she let go,
and reached down for her purse.

SMALL MIND
Centre Zen de la Main

> If your mind is related to something
> outside itself, that mind is a small
> mind.
>
> — Shunryu Suzuki

A bell sounds and everyone's still.
Outside, Saturday morning argues in French,
Portuguese. Big truck idles. Make that, huge truck.
Exhaust through the open window. Bird shadow
flits across the pine floor – that's more
like it. More like Big Mind. More like.
A noise, like crinkling paper, but organic.
At home, downstairs neighbours are moving to Victoria.
Taped boxes on the stairs read, *Christmas – Fragile.*
This side up. Mrs. K. says she's done nothing
but pack and throw up for two weeks – she's
lived here for sixty years, hates to *start over.*
What will move in? Rugby players who party
every Saturday night, smashed Molson Dry
bottles in the morning. Child's foot, dog's paw.
Someone here is wearing hair pomade, the kind
that comes in a royal blue glass jar, and smells
like bathroom deodorizer. I had some once,
and threw it out because the scent made me choke.
That sound again – a strange, soft bubbling, like
O_2 in a hospital room, or the way the human body
might sound if you could listen to the inside.
Listen to the inside. That sound is summer rain.

It's only been a week, and already
I have things I want to tell you.
How, for instance, I'm staring
into the same three-storey
building as when we last talked.
It's 4 p.m., and dark – close
to the shortest day of the year.
There's a convenience store
at street level and offices above.
Downstairs, the customers
come and go under overhead
fluorescents, into the bright
fishtank for magazines or
lotto tickets, back to the wet
slate soup of December.
The second floor has the same
lighting, and an open plan:
men and women run from desk
to desk all day, the light tubes burn late.
As you go up, through middle
management, to the top office
which belongs to the owner,
the lights get dimmer.
Upstairs there's only
a small man with a big desk,
several soft halogen lamps.
Sometimes, he practically lies
in his big reclining chair,
and shrieks into the speaker phone,
gesticulating wildly at the potted

palms and rubber trees.
I've seen him sit there
for most of a day and do
nothing but fiddle with his tie.
Then, as if he got the idea,
he'll punch the phone console:
a woman always comes.
Now he's packing his briefcase
with crisp folders, taking
his trenchcoat from the vestibule.
He adjusts the thermostat
and the room blacks out.
It isn't 5 p.m. yet, and the lower
floors still swarm with life.
The lights have gone out.
Those two black squares
were windows.

It's late enough in the afternoon sun
to chase my shadow home through the park,
much leaner and longer than me.

The soccer players crush each other
in slow motion, while a few solitary readers
look up from their benches.

A gull holds its curve in the air,
waiting for the right current
before it makes another move.

At dinner last night,
a young man with a broken arm
announced he'd slept for seven years.

Something like chronic fatigue:
he woke four months ago, nearly
thirty – everyone else was a lawyer.

It could have been the sun,
he said, but last weekend,
running for that frisbee,

the wooden picnic table dissolved.
He laughed and waved his cast
around and now I feel my stride lengthen

until I'm clipping my shadow's heels.
How long has it been? My jacket
fills with wind like a sail.

Tonight the sky's turned indigo
and the moon is secondhand.
When Kate was dying in August,
she'd bargain with the moon.
Now quarter, half or full, it's hers.

*

Hot dogs are out, since a Yellow cab
killed Bill as he crossed the street
for the taste of a really good one.
Papaya King, 72nd and Lex.

*

My grandfather collapsed in a bathroom,
gripping the sink for as long as he could.
Thirty years later, I watched his grand-niece
buy blue iris from a stand on St. Denis,
the summer of her last remission.
She was twenty-one and grinning
as she held the arrangement up.

*

A garden spade is what passed
between us at Kate's hillside burial,
and a vague sense of embarrassment,
as tendrils of fog whipped at our legs
like a scene from a Charles Addams cartoon.
Kate would have laughed. We cried.

*

Each of us dropped our spoonful
of earth – the box of ash inexplicably
still in its drawstring bag.
Someone took pictures but their camera
was stolen the following week in China.

*

A shovel is what Kate's nine-year-old
daughter asked for, and an adult to stay
behind with her until the ground was smooth.
Later, we ate cold meats, wine, good bread.
The child using her mother's hands.

Switch on the dorm's overhead lights
and in its small cage, a medium-sized
white rabbit will make a large display
of waking, as if the sleep has been long and deep.

It's been weeks since the sophomores
rolled their Nirvana posters, ten days
past the painters and their pails of fresh
white latex, longer since lettuce
was offered in the college cafeteria.

The rabbit will wince and wince at the glare.
This is natural. Through the delicate, scalloped
nostrils, twin brushstrokes above the mouth
like two pale treble clefs, its breath is negligible.

Your own breath will feel shortened, tight,
and you may begin to like it this way. But pry
that box of air towards your own body
as if cleaving a small drift, an eddy
from the field of snow the room's become.
You'll want to lie down. Don't.

Place the cage under an arm and feel
the rabbit's shudder in your neck.
Rabbits are supposed to be nervous,
which is why you must carry this one
down the dim corridor and push
that steel door open with your foot.

It may be like a car crash, violent
as birth. The world out there is full
of vegetables and noise. From here,
it looks like death. Wait. This is living.

III.

The Strange Familiar

The old couple rode their iceberg
farther and farther offshore from Florida,
while their grown children stood behind skyscraper
windows, barking corrections at them by phone.
The connections grew fainter and the children
lost their tempers – they were behind schedule,
thought the parents had removed their hearing aids
because they were irresponsible and wanted
to ruin their children's lives.
But the old people were laughing in bed
on their berg, cracking jokes they knew
fifteen or fifty years ago. It had grown so cold,
they no longer felt their pains – but they missed
home delivery of *The New York Times.*
And how, is what he'd have said, if anyone asked.
The old man kept going to the edge,
checking for the paper: nothing but water
in every direction. His wife stayed in bed, called
Circulation but she couldn't get through
because the children had tied up her line with
get up, get dressed and get some exercise,
with *you're not as far out as you think.*
Enough, is what I think she said,
before she flung the portable phone right off
the berg and crawled back under the duvet
to wait for her husband's return which,
presently, occurred. All the way down,
the phone told the fishes: *me, me, me.*

ABOUT THAT STOCKYARD

You were small and your father big.
Or was he nothing at all. The stockyard
was green or cropped bare,
the cattle gone to slaughter,
or crammed in an adjacent pen.

When a man tells his young son
how he longs for a homeland, does
the boy drag his feet, glance back
at the white house, sun-warmed flagstones,
yellow curtain in front, at his mother

in the garden, and wonder what
that *is?* Your father took your hand
when he told you these things.
You were almost a man, both
of you keeping your distance. The air
as clear as it gets on the Prairies.

Or was there dust in your mouth
as your father forged ahead, still
talking, and you hesitated, toes
clenched inside your sneakers,
cattle somewhere nearby? Their cries
were terrible. The silence is worse.

Afterwards, she likes to watch them go:
the anxious dry cleaner or the lawyer,
or the man she'd first seen selecting roses
from a sidewalk stall, his blunt, careful fingers.
She needs to watch them dress, restoring
their socks and important shoes,
to throw on something flimsy to see them off.
She loves their clatter in the stairwell,
their hidden skins carrying her traces
back to the world, the way her father
left for the plant every morning of his life,
her milky child's cheek against his rough one,
before his big boots hit the stairs running.
She takes in their backs, then the crowns
of receding hairlines, spiralling
to street level like specks to a sucking drain.
Her heart always flips once or twice
for her perfect, unreliable, stained men going.
She's left with her wanting intact,
whole in the stirred air, and no one
or nothing to pull her from the moment;
the way water vanished down the drain,
cold hands hauled her from the chair
she'd climbed to the kitchen sink,
saying, *Assez – c'est fini.*
The way her mother called her back
from the immense door, where she'd pressed
her whole bereft smallness, sniffing
her father and the outside air that took him:
Viens icitte, caline! Yé parti.

one of us asked, some night or day
when it still didn't matter whose back
was whose, when we didn't care who'd spoken.
One body, then two, caved in with laughter;
we lay there, shaking and helpless.

Didn't that command, anti-gravitational,
almost like prayer, hang in our shared air
for years? Who could rise to such heights?
Not him, not me, and our little private joke
got tired of waiting around.

Where's the tiny kneeling angel now,
goddess of the impossible, hovering
until the house of cards a coupling makes
collapses? Such desperate laughter.
I asked him to kneel in the air.

Montrose? So glad you've picked such a welcoming street.
Bobby Kennedy breathed, Pearson was Prime Minister,
when our black dachshund patrolled Montrose (in the days
when dogs had lives). He'd set out twice daily on rounds
of sniff and visit, close to the ground, straight down
Avenue Montrose, his own Rive Gauche, black nails clicking
and self-filing against the wide concrete walk, foot pads
calloused for the long haul, the sprinklers and cats of Montrose.
Winters, we worried over our man's tender equipment, dragged
through ice and salt, but Montrose always revealed our boulevardier
well before dinner, that eager four-stepping, petit flaneur – that black
tube with cracked yellow collar and clinking tags, reading, *Crackie.*
Westmount Dog. If lost, return me to that house, corner Montrose,
where someone is always home, waiting, willing to let you in.

ENTHUSIASM

>1. Possession by a god.
>
>— O.E.D.

What does it take to be happy? my friend
asks the single pay phone in Valhalla, B.C.,
her new, all-terrain vehicle parked outside.
She's quit her secure job for a man
she doesn't want to resist — a simpler life
with no power they can't generate themselves.

Here in a life that runs on time,
meeting Freud's criteria, meaning love,
meaning work — I stare down my desk
on this endless afternoon, and I don't
know what to say to her, except,
some mornings I long to break things.

Last night, blocks from here,
a huge crowd smashed plate glass and metal
because they'd *won* the Stanley Cup.
This apartment rocked as if storm-tossed,
while I watched a TV interview with a man
named Mario, who'd been stopped
by a reporter while throwing looted fruit:
I've waited seven years for this, he said
from inside Provigo's produce section,
and I feel very emotional right now.

Her first letters from B.C. were dizzy
with change, dappled with forest light,
the new man shining in the background
like a minor god. *I have what I wanted,*
she tells me now, *and it's not enough.*

By late last night, the riot
was only white noise in my apartment,
and when I woke in a heart-pounding panic
at 5 a.m., it was because of the sheer absence
of sound. I was rooting for your crazy scheme.
It has grown so quiet.

The second I slam my trunk, a black Jeep
in the next space starts its motor.
There is no driver in the vehicle,
no one else in the vast parking lot. The Jeep
must be ready to do something terrifying.
A blonde woman appears with controls.

At home, her cocktails pour themselves,
corn triangles fly into the chip dish,
salsa, to the matching bowl for dip.
The self-cleaning dog clips his leash
to his collar, while the oven warms
to the idea of the wrapped roast
she's tossed on the passenger seat.

From the car phone, she makes funeral
arrangements for the fourth husband,
though currently, she's still married
to the third. Above us, the autumn sun
starts failing for the day, resetting
itself for 6:49 a.m.

My cheap Chardonnay's stashed
in the trunk, a thin weed grows
through the pavement at my foot.
I must start my car with its key.
Drive.
There are no more surprises in the world.

SUMMER / ESTATÉ

(After Shirley Horn's version)

The first nectarine was less sweet
than its redness promised,
but the second, on the window's
white sill, has time and sunlight
moving over it, slow and sure
as the voice from the next room.

She hovers so long in the space
between words, between the piano's
chords, it seems she's lost it,
gone down in a tall field of summer,
given herself to the earth as a conduit
to our hearing, to summon a pleasure
so deep you're sure the woman will burst.

But she sings that ripeness over and over,
silence and juice, water and seed
and the patience – can it be learned? –
to let feeling rise to a fine spray of words,
notes from the throat, past the teeth,
a hiss so full of summer, of a lived
life you could close your hand around it.

You take the fruit with a single
motion: juice and sugars swarm
to the surface as you hold
the sun-warmed skin, as you lift it
to your open mouth, as you bite into
what you have waited for,
teeth sunk in summer's estate.

This beautiful black man, clearly gifted at his work,
and articulate, with a melodious (sorry, this is a fact)
island accent – the most magnificent man I've laid
eyes on in years, has just installed my new stove, and
we're talking about the Moroccan landlord, how badly
he treats the Quebecois janitor (*like an animal,* I say, and
he concurs). *He treats everyone badly*, I say, *he treats me
like a cow, because I'm a woman with no children – maybe it's
cultural,* I suggest, and, *has he insulted you, too?
Don't ask,* he says with a sigh, snapping the toolbox shut,
you really don't want to know, but his attention is fixed
on the next room, and the songs of a skinny white woman from
Austin, Texas, with a great mandolin player in her band,
and he says, *I really like your music,* and I say,
is there something you want me to sign?

When I heard about the twins who broke the casino,
I thought they were our neighbourhood familiars.
But the gamblers turned out to be men – in custody
until they prove they're masters of chaos theory, or luck.

Our twins are women, out today in the kind of outfits
zealous grandparents buy for tots. These two have
a matching enterprise, down to dual nose-rings, perfect
French braids. Yellow umbrellas rise when it rains.

Mornings at the Tabagie, each buys a *Journal de Montréal*,
an O'Henry bar, and waits for identical change. It's said
that they read in a café down the street, two strange flowers,
turning the pages of their personal newspapers in synch.

Who speaks first? I'm told there is no need for speech.
Now, they stroll in floral raincoats and pink pants.
People turn, stare. Matched steps are maintained.
Look, all you solitaries, say the cabbage-rose earrings.

We're completely understood, say the pony-fur purses.
The day we were born, our parents said they'd broken the bank,
says the flash of green silk scarves. Do they have jobs?
I think not. They are too rich in pleasure. Lucky. Lucky.

I am the odourless gas seeping up from the cellar to fold
you and your children in my arms and take you down.

I am the car that comes from nowhere, just as your dog
recognizes the dog across the street and runs for it.

I am every interruption between here and there, every
dreaded phone call, leak in your heart, snag in your stocking.

I am your sensitive tooth, the worn enamel, the nerve.
I am the woman with her elbows on your kitchen table

across from the man you love and want to trust.
The three of us are eating nachos. He leans forward.

> At any given time, all the male humpbacks singing
> in the North Atlantic are singing essentially the
> same song.... So much promiscuous sex for a species
> verging on the edge of extinction is encouraging.
> — Erich Hoyt, *Seasons of the Whale*

was the story he told her after they'd first met – more
a description, really, of a movie on whale song and courtship –
as they trawled one long block of Chinatown for parking.

The streets looked bombed as usual for a cold night
in February, and a billboard offering discount flights
dwarfed the last Buddhist church left on Viger.

As they circled, he kept coming back to exactly
how the world's largest mammals make love
in their element – so huge, musical, so impossibly gentle.

They found parking; there was talk over Arborite tables
and bowls of good Vietnamese soup.
The whole block burned down the following month,

but there was no future when they circled
at the end of winter. Next morning, making coffee
at home, she recognized his story as song.

Would she still have answered him, knowing
how abruptly the singing ended, how
the ashes of Viger Street go on smoking? Yes.

NOTICE TO CUT TREE

This week in the country, I've run
on dirt roads, where select trees
have numbers posted on their trunks,
and the small print urges interested parties
to a meeting on each tree's future.
I've grown attached to tree twenty-seven,
want to stay, discuss it with the tree warden.

How quickly we make the strange familiar,
the places we're known in, remote.
The town meeting on the poster took place
a month ago, and I have one night left here.
This afternoon, I open the doors
to the slanting light, the field mouse
I woke to on my pillow, resolute skunk,
snazzy as a spectator shoe, who pitched and reeled
along the road to a Richard Thompson tune,
until I jumped into the ditch, and let him pass.

This afternoon, I sit on the front step,
offer my arm to the mosquito, my ankle
to the swollen black fly; the mice can come
and make their beds here – and to the wind,
which needs nothing from me, I say, *tree, tree.*

IV.

The Bottle Picker's Progress

✳

We'd argued that night, there'd been tears, and as the car pulled out,
the only sounds were our seat-belt tongues, clicking into their holders.

Then a shout, and a dapper man in a good suit, probably sixty-five,
ran over, one hand high, and spoke into his tiny, folding phone:

Nancy, I've found a space, just drive around the corner,
look left, I'm here – I'm holding it. And you, always the patient,

kind one, always quick to laugh, just drove away from how
his face lit that patch of claimed asphalt, expecting her Camry.

And I drove away with you, unable to look, convinced
that Nancy was breaking the speed limit in the other direction,

heading for uncharted neighbourhoods in her luxury car, her
small, veined hands clamped to the wheel, that even if the man

stood there all night, punching numbers into the phone, Nancy
had other plans, Nancy was out of here, Nancy had gone downtown.

We were sitting near the door at Bistro Quatre,
when a scrofulous man appeared, pressed
a tiger lily on each woman at the table,
turned to our one man for money.
Spotlit, across the room, someone
was reading prose poems about her abusive father –
how he sliced the legs from live frogs,
and died, too. Her pain was uncut.

We tried to hand the flowers back,
but he pushed them at us, grasping
for money with a hand missing fingers.
He pocketed the coins without speaking, tore
the bloom from his last lily and flung it
toward the woman at the mike – who was saying,
I believe, that he touched her *here*, something
with a knife, that she hates her father most for dying.

Our man rubbed the entreé, from the bistro's blackboard,
and loped out as quickly as he'd come, leaving
the soup, a smear, and dessert. I remember
little else from that night, which went on
too long, the flowers dying slowly on the table.
But when we spilled from the bar, expecting dark,
it was into the bright wash of a city's full moon,
and at its centre, the galloping man, crisscrossing
Boulevard St. Laurent, making revisions at bar
after bar, as if at last, he hoped to get it right.

From the yard, we watch her watch us,
her smooth skull having loosed the beauty
of her face. These last weeks, she's told me,
are clear, her hold on what is good and beautiful
about this life, fierce – such a far cry
from how she'd thought to live before.

Her husband is building a stone wall
dug deep into this earth, comes home
to heave one, maybe two rocks an evening.
This growth will be slower than bonsai.
He has finished the foundations, the three
wide steps to the kitchen door, where she stands,
the big dog curled at her feet, tail thumping.

I can't tell this man if we dig deeper
in Quebec than he does in upstate New York, never
having had land to fence, never having thought of it.
Now she gazes at our strong bodies, brushed
with late sun, and I lose the details
of frostline and mortar: I watch him
climb the hill to her, follow her inside.

I keep the dog with me, his old head
between my hands, sit on the cold stone
until the chill deepens and I have to stand.
The dog runs in crazed – oh dog joy!
– circles, and flings himself against me,
asking for comfort: I slide my hands along
his ribs until I hold his pounding heart.

Just back from California this early Sunday,
and now, those introspective singer-songwriters, or Bach,
even the manic genius of Glenn Gould – just won't cut it.
Outside, in the gentle Montreal morning
of my childhood, an old man shuffles past
on the arm of his paid, young companion.
Pink impatiens do what they do in orderly beds,
as the odd cyclist zips by in black-and-white Spandex
under Sherbrooke Street's arched maples.
A homeless man, his hand out for change, seems
tentative, almost apologetic. In San Francisco,
I heard someone tell a panhandler, 'Sorry man,
but change comes from within.' Yes, that's
a non sequitur, and neighbours, I'm sorry.
But this moth on the window screen is too grey
and plain to me, after driving the fire-seared hills
of Oakland, after crossing the Bay Bridge
to the city at nightfall, as banked fog moved,
like pure violet cataclysm across the navy bay.
Neighbours, this calls for Peter Gabriel,
his overblown synthesizers, overlaid drum tracks.
Neighbours, we live like orderly mice here
atop the Laurentian fault, Precambrian
and deep as the San Andreas. Surely, this
calls for a brighter noise. I'm sorry, neighbours –
you, concert pianist; you, sleepy optician;
you, McGill phys. ed. coach with the girlfriend,
here only on weekends – I'm sorry. But the man
I love sleeps on his side in that other landscape,
fog stalled over the city, as Sandburg said, on cat's feet.

Here, our papers fill with fights over the language
of signs, instead of what they signify. I'm sorry,
neighbours, to wake you from pleasant or anxious
dreams, but the very limestone under your beds
is grinding against itself right now (for God's
sake, I could have put on Wagner's marches!),
and this building settled on its foundations
nearly one hundred years ago and trembles
with every bus that goes by. Neighbours,
I'm sorry about all this bass and percussion
so early on a Sunday, but hey – d'you *feel* that?

Our new neighbour holds court in the dim stairwell.
Coming and going, I climb over her mug
and ashtray, as she tells the portable phone:
Three months ago, you said I was your strength.
Where is this coming from – what's going on?

She is going to argue this one, and any
passerby could tell her it's futile.
But for now, she plans strategy, moves
her pins around the salt-stained stair –
mug, ashtray, ashtray, mug.

All day the hall smells of smoke and perfume,
all day she's in conference.
Outside, spring explodes, weeks ahead
of schedule, and a man who doesn't
want her now is out there, in it.

By summer, she'll have forgotten
how she built herself a sanctuary.
There'll be a vague memory of pleading,
a sharper one of incomprehension,
and maybe, just the shape of his absence.

For now she holds court, digging herself
as far in or out of the world
as a person can get: once you've
been there it stays in your cells – you're
gone without leaving the building.

At the edge of sleep, I thought it was snow
I heard brush and rattle the bay windows;
the same hour when cars glide soundlessly
down white Montreal streets and the smell
of winter creeps around window frames,
straight under doors into dreams.
But our baby is now the size of a lima bean
and growing fast in this place where winter
means red bottle brushes dangling from trees
and crazy-fragile freesias in street vendors' buckets.
I must have curled myself around our bean
like a thick seed coating against the cold,
and I was glad to do so, though when I woke,
way, way down in the bed, small as I could
make myself, what I heard in this clear, indigo
midnight, was the bottle-picker's progress
among our block's blue boxes, and it was
a minor miracle that the empties could rattle so
in a grocery cart filling with snow.

CONFECTION

Who else should paint San Francisco, but this man
whose reputation includes large canvases
of cream pies, tea cakes, triangular
party sandwiches of egg, salmon and cheese?

How else to explain this rippling grid of streets
clinging to hills as something you want to lick?
Victorian houses are stacked like chalky pastel
mints, the pavement's a ribbon of licorice.

Even a tiered bank building is frosted
thick as wedding cake, melting in the sun.
There are no people in his landscapes.
Just schematic power lines for streetcars overdue,

and an occasional dog as a speck – like a fly
or a currant – shaken loose from the palette knife's
cream. Everyone must be inside double parlours
in Wayne Thiebaud's San Francisco.

Their bodies are so filled with absorbed light,
they are bursting around a pink cloth,
from which they have eaten the last of a cake.
A man goes to his window, licks his lips,

finds one sweet crumb and swallows.
Below him, a woman is walking in the street.
She is new to such abundance, wants to walk
until the last light is sucked from the sky.

The man stands, a pink napkin in his hand.
The woman glances up, then continues on her way.
What, she wants to ask the man, *is going
on here? I've never been so hungry in my life.*

Acknowledgements:

Thanks to the places where these poems were first printed or broadcast: *arc; Brick; Carousel; Celidih; The Literary Review of Canada; The Malahat Review; Ms.; The New Yorker*; CBC Radio's *Morningside*; CKUT Radio's *Wired on Words*. To The Canada Council for a grant that aided in their completion. To the sharp hearts and minds at Brick Books, and those of Montreal's Tuesday Night Group. To my friends and family on both sides of the border, *je vous remerçie.* Lewis and Maddy, *te amo*.

Notes:

'A Bus in Nova Scotia': several lines here are direct adaptations from the poetry or prose of Elizabeth Bishop.

'About That Stockyard' is for Mark Abley.

Julie Bruck's first book, *The Woman Downstairs*, received QSPELL's A.M. Klein Award in 1994. Her recent work won a National Magazine Award for poetry, and has appeared in such magazines as *Carousel, Ceilidh, Ms.*, and *The New Yorker*. A native Montrealer, she has taught writing at Concordia University, and has been a regular contributor to CBC Radio. She lives in San Francisco, California.